To: _____

From: _____

Date: _____

Celebrating Christmas

It's a quiet night,
The sky is clear,
The stars are shining bright.
It is the night
of Jesus' birth
God has sent His Light.

Foretold by prophets
long ago
The story now fulfilled
The Savior's come
by virgin birth.
A weary world is stilled.

Ages before the birth of Christ, the prophets of old were led by God to reveal the coming of a great Messiah:

And she shall bring forth a son, and thou shalt call his name JESUS: for he shall save his people from their sins. Now all this was done, that it might be fulfilled which was spoken of the Lord by the prophet, saying, "Behold, a virgin shall be with child, and shall bring forth a son, and they shall call his name Immanuel, which being interpreted is, God with us."

Matthew 1:21

Born in Bethlehem

But thou, Bethlehem Ephratah, though thou be little among the thousands of Judah, yet out of thee shall he come forth unto me that is to be ruler in Israel; whose goings forth have been from of old, from everlasting.

Micah 5:2

O little town of Bethlehem, how still we see thee lie!
Above thy deep and dreamless sleep the silent stars go by.
Yet in thy dark streets shineth the everlasting Light;
The hopes and fears of all the years are met in thee tonight.

"O Little Town of Bethlehem"

Born of a Virgin

Therefore the Lord himself shall give you a sign;
Behold, a virgin shall conceive, and bear a son,
and shall call his name Immanuel.

Isaiah 7:14

But while he thought on these things, behold, the angel
of the LORD appeared unto him in a dream, saying,
Joseph, thou son of David, fear not to take unto thee
Mary thy wife: for that which is conceived in her is of
the Holy Ghost. And she shall bring forth a son, and
thou shalt call his name JESUS, for he shall save his
people from their sins.

Matthew 1:20-21

And he said unto them, "These are the words which I spake unto you, while I was yet with you, that all things must be fulfilled, which were written in the law of Moses, and in the prophets, and in the psalms, concerning me."

Luke 24:44

[And Jesus said,] "Think not that I am come to destroy the law, or the prophets: I am not come to destroy, but to fulfill."

Matthew 5:17

And when thy days be fulfilled, and thou shalt sleep with thy fathers, I will set up thy seed after thee and I will establish his kingdom.

2. Samuel 7:12

Now when Jesus was born in Bethlehem of
Judea in the days of Herod the king,
behold, there came wise men
from the east to Jerusalem.

Matthew 2:1

*And there were in the same country
shepherds abiding in the field, keeping
watch over their flock by night.*

Luke 2:8

And, lo, the star, which they saw in the east, went before them, till it came and stood over where the young child was.

Matthew 2:9

When they saw the star, they rejoiced with exceeding great joy.

Matthew 2:10

Led by the light of a brilliant star, the wise
men found the Christ child on that quiet
night long ago. We can still find Him today, if
only we take the time to look.

Just as they were led by the Heavenly Father,
so are we led today. Not by a star, but by the
Light of Christ. Each night and day His
words are a guide to us.

And by the light of that same star,

Three wise men came from country afar.

To seek for a King was their intent,

And to follow the star wherever it went.

While shepherds kept their watching,
O'er silent flocks by night,
Behold throughout the heavens,
There shone a holy light

"Go Tell it on the Mountain"

Behold, the angel of the Lord appeareth to Joseph in a dream, saying, "Arise, and take the young child and his mother, and flee into Egypt, and be thou there until I bring thee word."

Matthew 2:13

Chosen by God for a special purpose, Mary
and Joseph were called upon to take a journey.
It was a journey of faith, and they trusted the
Lord and followed.

We will experience many journeys throughout
our own lives with different paths to follow
and many choices to make. There will be
times when we are called upon to act with
faith. And — just as Mary and Joseph found
— we can be sure that the hand of God will
show us the way.

Joy to the world!
The Lord is come!

And she brought forth her firstborn son, and wrapped him in swaddling clothes, and laid him in a manger.

Luke 2:7

And this shall be a sign unto you. Ye shall find the babe wrapped in swaddling clothes, lying in a manger.

Luke 2:12

And in the sixth month the angel Gabriel was sent from God unto a city of Galilee, named Nazareth, to a virgin espoused to a man whose name was Joseph, of the house of David; and the virgin's name was Mary. And the angel came in unto her, and said, "Hail, thou that art highly favored, the Lord is with thee: blessed art thou among women." And when she saw him, she was troubled at his saying, and cast in her mind what manner of salutation this should be. And the angel said unto her, "Fear not, Mary: for thou hast found favor with God. And, behold, thou shalt conceive in thy womb, and bring forth a son, and shalt call his name Jesus."

Luke 1:26-31

Come adore on bended knee,
Christ the Lord, the newborn King.

"Angels We Have Heard on High"

Where is He that is born King of the Jews?
For we have seen His star in the east,
and are come to worship Him.

Matthew 2:1-2

And it came to pass in those days, that there went out a decree from Caesar Augustus that all the world should be taxed. And all went to be taxed, every one into his own city. And Joseph also went up from Galilee, out of the city of Nazareth, into Judea, unto the city of David, which is called Bethlehem, to be taxed with Mary, his espoused wife, being great with child. And so it was, that, while they were there, the days were accomplished that she should be delivered.

And she brought forth her firstborn son, and wrapped him in swaddling clothes, and laid him in a manger; because there was no room for them in the inn.

Luke 2:1-7

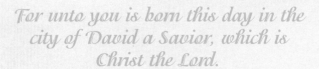

For unto you is born this day in the city of David a Savior, which is Christ the Lord.

Luke 2:11

Down in a lowly manger,
Our humble Christ was born.
And God sent us salvation
that blessed Christmas morn.

"Go Tell it on the Mountain"

What a glorious night! Foretold by prophets and angels, the blessed night had finally come. Visited by angels, Mary and Joseph learned of the plan God had for them. But God's high and holy purpose would be carried out in very simple fashion.

The King of Kings would not enter the world with men sounding trumpets. He would not be born in a golden palace, holding a scepter. The rich and famous would not attend His birth. No engraved birth announcements would go out with the news.

The brilliant light of a simple star would note his coming. He would be born in a lowly barn. Instead of trumpets, His arrival would be heralded by the voices of angels. Humble shepherds would be in attendance.

You may have noticed in your life that God sometimes uses the simplest means to affect the greatest things. Just as He chose very humble circumstances for the birth of His Son, He sometimes chooses very rudimentary means to bring things into our lives.

Perhaps you prayed for money; what you really needed was a friend. Perhaps you asked God for a new job, but He blessed someone else's life by keeping you where you were.

Just remember, even though we can't always see the meaning in certain events, it doesn't mean that God doesn't have a grand and glorious plan behind it.

"He shall be great, and shall be called the Son
of the Highest; and the Lord God shall give
unto him the throne of his father David. And
he shall reign over the house of Jacob for ever;
and of his kingdom there shall be no end."

Then said Mary unto the angel, "How shall this
be, seeing I know not a man?" And the angel
answered and said unto her, "The Holy Ghost
shall come upon thee, and the power of the
Highest shall overshadow thee: therefore also
that holy thing which shall be born of thee
shall be called the Son of God."

Luke 1:32-35

The shepherds said one to another, "Let us now go even unto Bethlehem, and see this thing which is come to pass, which the Lord hath made known unto us."

Luke 2:15

From God our heavenly Father
A blessed angel came.
And unto certain shepherds,
Brought tidings of the same.

"God Rest Ye Merry Gentlemen"

And the shepherds returned, glorifying and praising God for all the things that they had heard and seen, as it was told unto them.

Luke 2:20

The first Noel the angels did say,
Was to certain poor shepherds in
fields where they lay.
In fields where they lay keeping their sheep,
On a cold winter's night that was so deep.

"The First Noel"

The Christmas season has always been about visitors. Whether angels or the wise men of old, God has a habit of sending the right people to the right place at the right time. God may not guide you with a star, but if you listen carefully, you will hear His voice. His Spirit will guide you.

As you celebrate the birth of the Savior, rejoice in the love of your family and friends. Take comfort in the company of the visitors God has sent you and give thanks for the glorious gift of Jesus Christ.

Hark! The herald angels sing
Glory to the newborn King!

"Hark! The Herald Angels Sing"

What child is this, who laid to rest
On Mary's lap is sleeping?
Whom angels greet with anthems sweet
While shepherds watch are keeping.

"What Child is This?"

Behold, the angel of the LORD appeared unto him in a dream, saying, "Joseph, thou son of David, fear not to take unto thee Mary thy wife: for that which is conceived in her is of the Holy Ghost."

Matthew 1:20

Glories stream from heaven afar.
Heavenly hosts sing alleluia.
Christ the Savior is born!
Christ the Savior is born!

"Silent Night"

And, lo, the angel of the Lord came
upon them,
and the glory of the Lord shone
round about them;
and they were sore afraid.
And the angel said unto them,
"Fear not: for, behold,
I bring you good tidings of great joy,
which shall be to all people."

Luke 2:9-10

Come to Bethlehem and see,
Him whose birth the angels sing.

"Angels We Have Heard on High"

The world in solemn stillness lay,
To hear the angels sing.

"It Came Upon the Midnight Clear"

And when they were come into the house,
they saw the young child with Mary his
mother, and fell down,
and worshipped him:
and when they had opened their treasures,
they presented unto him gifts;
gold and frankincense and myrrh.

Matthew 2:11

Why did the wise men bring gifts to Jesus? After all, as the King of Kings and Lord of Lords, He certainly had no need of earthly gifts. Gold, frankincense and myrrh were presented to the Christ child not because He had need of them, but because the wise men had need of the Savior.

The wise men had studied the scriptures. They knew the words of the prophets that foretold the coming Messiah. They recognized the signs. Because of who the Child was, the men were compelled to worship Him and to honor him with precious gifts.

What gift will you bring to Jesus this Christmas season? After all, it is His birthday you're celebrating. Why not give Him the gift of yourself? What else do you have to give?

They entered in those wise men three,
Full reverently, upon bended knee.
And offered there, in His presence,
Their gold and myrrh
and frankincense.

"The First Noel"

How silently, how silently
the wondrous gift is given.
So God imparts to human hearts
the blessings of His heaven.

"O, Little Town of Bethlehem"

What gift will you give to family and friends
this holiday season? Whether it's a quickly
chosen scarf and gloves or a well-thought-
out gift they will long treasure, nothing can
compare to the gift of time spent with
those you love.

Don't lose sight of the true meaning of the
Christmas season. It's not about how much
money you spend. It's not about the pretty
paper and bows. It's about the love behind
the gift. Most importantly, it's about the
greatest gift ever given.

We often say that great things come in small
packages. Just think of the wondrous gift
that God gave us in the form of a wee babe.

Finished with your Christmas shopping?
Christmas decorations all in place?
Still planning the menu for your holiday feast?

During the hustle and bustle of the holiday season, it's easy to become overwhelmed by all of the activity. Shopping soon becomes a chore, and the meaning of this blessed occasion is lost. This Christmas, take the time to hear God's voice and to follow His words.

And remember, the greatest gift you receive this Christmas will not be anything wrapped in a package. In fact, it's a gift you've already received. It is the blessed gift that God sent us more than 2,000 years ago. It is God's love in the form of His Son, Jesus Christ.

This holiday season, make it your goal to keep Christ in Christmas. As you're wrapping presents and exchanging gifts, take the time to reflect upon the greatest gift of all. After all, Jesus really is the reason for the season.

But the gift of God is eternal life through
Jesus Christ our Lord.

Romans 6:23

Joy, joy for Christ is born.
The Babe, the Son of Mary.

"What Child is This?"

A thrill of hope,
The weary world rejoices.
For yonder breaks a new and
glorious morn!

"Oh Holy Night"